"Therefore I tell you, do not be anxious about your life... But seek first the Kingdom of God and His righteousness, and all these things will be added to you."

MATTHEW 6:25-33

Celebrate Salvation!®

Kingdom
God's Reign in our Midst
Realm E - His Kingdom, here now and forever

The Joy of Christian Discipleship Series
Book 6

Dr. Bill Morehouse

His Kingdom Press

About Dr. Bill Morehouse

Dr. Morehouse was raised in a traditional Christian home in the 1950's and functionally became a humanist during college and medical school in the 1960's. After completing his medical residency in Family Medicine in the early 1970's he embarked on a career of serving the poor but soon found that his secular faith and alternative lifestyle were woefully inadequate to the task.

In 1974 he underwent a dramatic conversion from the philosophy and lifestyle he had been living to a wholehearted commitment to Jesus as his Lord and Savior. After returning to medicine and marrying in 1975, he and his wife dedicated themselves to growing in faith, raising their family of four children (plus spouses and grandchildren), and providing Christ-centered service to some of the most disadvantaged members of their community.

Since retiring from active clinical practice in July 2018, Dr. Morehouse has devoted himself to continued Christian growth, family, study, writing, and teaching about the Kingdom of God. He has had long personal and professional experience with the material covered in Celebrate Salvation.®

Kingdom: God's Reign in our Midst

Copyright 2022 by William R. Morehouse
ISBN: 978-1-7353899-6-7 (paperback)
Web Address: www.celebratesalvation.org

His Kingdom Press
Rochester, New York 14619

Special discounts are available on quantity purchases by corporations, associations, educators, and others. For details, contact the publisher through www.hiskingdom.us/press.

Kingdom Contents

Acknowledgements

The work you have in your hands is part of a deeply rooted and ongoing collaboration that extends back for generations and even millennia. Jesus came to reveal God's love to struggling mankind and to demonstrate the depth of that love in ways that have had a profound impact on countless lives and entire societies ever since. He embodied the fullness of God in human form and called us out of darkness, confusion, and bondage into the wonderful light, clarity, and freedom we were created to inhabit.

We start out so fresh and pure as infants but soon become soiled and spoiled. Then as the years go by we get deeper and deeper into life's inevitable corruptions. As the Psalmist wrote:

> *The* LORD *looks down from heaven on the children of man, to see if there are any who understand, who seek after God. They have all turned aside; together they have become corrupt; there is none who does good, not even one.*
>
> Psalm 14:2-3, also noted in Psalm 53:1-3 and Romans 3:10-12

Can we reverse this process and become clean again? Do you believe in second, third, and even seven times seventieth chances? God does.

Historically, there were entire eras when certain troubling human conditions like discrimination, injustice, and poverty, were just written off as hopeless. This work owes a deep debt of gratitude to the God who saves, fellow believers in the Body of Christ, and others who have been and are working tirelessly to reveal and share the truth that God hears our prayers and is patiently revealing His Kingdom in our midst, within our hearts and around us in our communities.

Many people are continuing to contribute their prayers, thoughts, ideas, and constructive comments to the growth and development of Celebrate Salvation.® I am particularly grateful to the pioneering work of generations of those who have gone before me as well as to many contributors in my local church fellowship and beyond. I would especially like to honor my wife and life partner, Susan, for her unfailing love and support over the decades we have been given to share life, faith, family, and community together.

Meeting 21ˢᵗ Century Needs, Part 2

We are increasingly living in an age of confusion about truth and falsehood. Who is telling the truth, and can we really tell the difference? Enlightenment misunderstandings about the governments of men and of God, Postmodernism, Eastern mysticism, blurred messaging in the faith community, questions about life after death and the reality of heaven and hell, and the blending of secular with spiritual definitions of terms like freedom, liberty, and justice… What does our faith have to offer? As the prophet noted,

Justice is turned back, and righteousness stands far away; for truth has stumbled in the public squares, and uprightness cannot enter.   Isaiah 59:14

In an attempt to address the need for guidance that an increasing number are searching for, Celebrate Salvation® has developed a broad-based Christ-centered study series and discipleship program designed to reach a wide audience of sincere seekers. Are you yearning for truth in our troubled age, a new believer seeking to be established in your faith, someone who has recently renewed your faith commitment in Christ and wants to revitalize your faith and ability to be an effective witness to others, or a church leader committed to equipping your congregation for growth? If so, our courses may help you find what you are seeking.

Celebrate Salvation's® underlying design began with a time-honored set of biblical steps to living faith very clearly outlined during a time of revival in the early 20ᵗʰ Century by the Oxford Group. One outgrowth of this movement became the well-known 12-Steps and Traditions of AA which have been instrumental in helping millions find God-given strength to overcome addictive behaviors. In the 1990s the 12-Step approach was significantly reframed by John Baker and Rick Warren at Saddleback Church into a clearly Christian program called Celebrate Recovery® (CR) which is compatible with its Oxford Group roots and applicable to a wider array of common human difficulties.

Over the years, many have observed that Step programs capture the essential and lifelong biblical dynamics involved in becoming a spiritually born-again believer and active disciple of Jesus Christ. Sadly, apart from programs like AA and CR, struggles with pornography and other negative or destructive attitudes or behaviors that impair many people's lives are often not covered in church gatherings, pulpit

Background Material

messages, or new member classes. Perhaps it's because people may be reluctant to be open about potentially embarrassing problems or congregations may lack the capacity to handle them. Access to faith-based Christian growth and discipleship resources for helping members and new believers overcome personal issues and become solidly established in their faith may also be limited.

Many of us also find ourselves aching for an outpouring of God's Holy Spirit, for times of widespread revival and spiritual awakening. Are we prepared? What would happen if God were to answer our prayers and pour out His Spirit throughout our communities, breaking open those already in the church and bringing in a large influx of new believers laden with the issues of our modern world? Would we and our churches know how to handle a Great Awakening like this? Celebrate Salvation® has taken the Oxford Group's steps, as modified by 12-Step and CR programs, and clarified them further with grateful credit to make them available to the church at large in a series of study guides organized into two courses and a devotional as listed on Page 61.

Course 1: Established in 3 Stages (A, B, C) and 7 Steps builds on the work of the Oxford Group and covers the foundational process of becoming established as a disciple of Jesus who is saved by His grace, committed to ongoing sanctification, and ready to live out His Great Commission with purity, integrity, and enthusiasm.

Course 2: Equipped in 3 Realms (D, E, F) and 7 Understandings goes beyond the foundational studies of Course 1 by helping group members understand how to cooperate with God as He brings spiritual awakening to individuals, churches, and entire communities; advances His Kingdom in our midst; and continually undergirds us with assurances about our future beyond the grave as well as between now and then.

Discovering the ever-unfolding mystery of faith in the living God is a wonderfully profound, life-changing, and satisfying gift. Our hope is that this modest series of introductory studies will provide a biblically balanced and comprehensive understanding of our faith which is widely applicable, reproducible, and fruitful. Please use the materials in *The Joy of Christian Discipleship Series* and augment them with those of your own fellowship group as we seek to meet the needs of our time with God's faithful Word.

Dr. Bill Morehouse
August 2022

Meeting 21ˢᵗ Century Needs, Part 2

Celebrate Salvation!®
The Joy of Christian Discipleship Course 2
Equipped in 3 Realms with 7 Understandings

Awakening: The Triumph of Truth
D - Waking up into the Light of God

1. **Natural birth and growth:** The processes of birth, becoming aware and oriented, growing, learning, and maturing through the natural stages of life.

2. **Spiritual birth and discipleship:** Similarities between natural growth processes and those of spiritual rebirth, awakening to spiritual realities, and growing in discipleship.

3. **Awakening of faith in communities:** The dynamics and social consequences of spiritual awakening in groups and broader segments of society.

Kingdom: God's Reign in our Midst
E - His Kingdom, here now and forever

4. **What is a kingdom?** Understanding where we fit in the authority and social structures around us, including models of family, church, community, education, industry, and government.

5. **Our dual citizenship:** How to live fruitful lives simultaneously in the temporal kingdoms of this world and the everlasting Kingdom of God.

6. **The Millennial Kingdom and beyond:** Anticipating Christ's second coming, millennial reign, and final judgment while living in the realities of today's world.

Heaven: Our Ultimate Destiny
F - Living faithful lives into eternity

7. **Our eternal home:** Casting a vision of where we will be after we die and how we can live our lives between now and then. The **Destination**, **Transition**, and **Journey**.

Background Material

4

About Course 2

Similar to the material in Course 1 of *The Joy of Christian Discipleship Series*, **Course 2** has been developed as three books to complete our series: the first is about the ***Awakening*** of living faith, the second our citizenships in the world and the ***Kingdom*** of God, and the third our ultimate destiny as inheritors of eternal life extending into ***Heaven***. These workbooks are designed to serve as study guides for individuals or small discipleship groups of 2-10 (ideal 3-7) committed members. Each of the three studies can be completed in about 12 weekly sessions over one semester or 3-month period with breaks for holidays.

The material in **Course 2** is presented in a somewhat denser writing style and overlaps and goes beyond that found in Course 1. As such, the course can stand alone and be studied either before or after Course 1 by relatively new believers, long-standing believers, or even members of churches who might not consider themselves to be "evangelical" in their focus or traditional affiliations. New groups may gather and start at any time with motivated leaders who have good reputations in their local churches. Unlike Course 1 which relies on having separate groups for men and women to preserve safe sharing of sensitive personal subjects, **Course 2** content can be handled well by mixed groups.

Each of the three **Course 2** guides is divided into twelve 4-page weekly interactive lessons – four lessons on each of the three Understandings in the first two guides and four lessons on Journey, Transition, and Destination in the third and final guide. Supplementary handouts designed to accompany each study guide in the series are available at www.celebratesalvation.org/more/#2 or in a companion book.

Kingdom: God's Reign in our Midst moves from individual and more widespread awakening into the realm of God's authority, from being our Savior to reigning as our King. This study addresses three questions: How do the earthly "kingdoms" we interact with compare with God's heavenly Kingdom? What is the *"good news of the Kingdom of God"* that Jesus proclaimed and demonstrated in power throughout His earthly ministry? And what is our place in God's unfolding plan?

For he said to them, "I must preach the good news of the Kingdom of God to the other towns as well; for I was sent for this purpose." Luke 4:43

Discipleship Course 2 Design

Course 2 Group Guidelines

1. Prepare for each meeting by reading the week's lesson and writing down some notes about each question in advance.
2. Try to keep your group sharing focused on your own thoughts, feelings, experiences, and insights about each question. Limit your sharing to allow room for group discussion.
3. Please avoid cross-talk. Cross-talk is when two people engage in side conversations during the meeting that exclude others. Each person is free to express their own feelings without interruptions.
4. Remember that we are here to support one another, not to instruct, preach at, or "fix" one another.
5. Anonymity and confidentiality are essential requirements in a trusting discipleship group. Personal information that is shared in the group stays in the group.
6. Offensive or demeaning language has no place in a Christian fellowship group.
7. Please silence your personal electronic devices and put them aside.

Suggestions for Course 2 Group Leadership

Unlike the first two studies in Course 1, mixed groups are acceptable in all Course 2 studies. Schedule regular weekly meetings to last about 90 minutes. Ensure participants have study guides and access to handouts.

1. Gather group in a circle and open meeting on time with prayer and brief comments about group business and upcoming events.
2. Go around circle with introductions including first name in early group meetings, brief status of faith, and personal concerns for prayer.
3. Continue around the circle by sequentially reading the 3 Realms and 7 Understandings and the Group Guidelines for the first few meetings, then one of the Confessional Prayers in unison at every group meeting.
4. Start each lesson by reading the introductory paragraphs around the circle and then opening with the first question.
5. Keep group sharing within Guidelines.
6. Circulate basket for prayer requests; then recirculate so each person who submitted one can take a different one home for intercession.
7. Bring copies of next week's handouts to pass out in advance.
8. Close meeting on time with prayer, allowing members to linger for conversation for a while. Refreshments optional.

Background Material

Confession and Prayer

The 23rd Psalm

The LORD is my shepherd; I shall not want. He makes me lie down in green pastures. He leads me beside still waters. He restores my soul. He leads me in paths of righteousness for his name's sake. Even though I walk through the valley of the shadow of death, I will fear no evil, for you are with me; your rod and your staff, they comfort me. You prepare a table before me in the presence of my enemies; you anoint my head with oil; my cup overflows. Surely goodness and mercy shall follow me all the days of my life, and I shall dwell in the house of the LORD forever.

David

The Lord's Prayer

"Our Father in heaven, hallowed be YOUR NAME. Your Kingdom come, Your will be done on earth as it is in heaven. Give us this day our daily bread, and forgive us our sins, as we forgive those who sin against us. Do not lead us into temptation, but deliver us from the evil one, for Yours is the Kingdom and the power and the glory forever. Amen."

Jesus

The Serenity Prayer

God, grant me the serenity to accept the things I cannot change, the courage to change the things I can, and the wisdom to know the difference. Living one day at a time, enjoying one moment at a time; accepting hardship as a pathway to peace; taking, as Jesus did, this sinful world as it is, not as I would have it; trusting that You will make all things right if I surrender to Your will; so that I may be reasonably happy in this life and supremely happy with You forever in the next. Amen.

Reinhold Niebuhr

What a Wonderful World!

O Lord, how manifold are your works! In wisdom have you made them all; the earth is full of your creatures. Here is the sea, great and wide, which teems with creatures innumerable, living things both small and great. There go the ships, and Leviathan, which you formed to play in it.   Psalm 104:24-26

I see trees of green, red roses too; I see them bloom for me and you, and I think to myself, "What a wonderful world!"

I see skies of blue and clouds of white; the bright blessed day, the dark sacred night, and I think to myself, "What a wonderful world!"

Louis Armstrong 1967

Our world is truly full of amazing wonders, both natural and man-made. Consider the progress we've made as human beings just in the past century in communication, production, and technology – the wonders of wireless transmission, transportation, agriculture, and medicine. We've shrunk the world, searched the galaxies, and sent people to the moon. We've conquered smallpox and subdued AIDS. Along the way we've embraced untold numbers of falsehoods, learned how to incinerate entire cities and, not to be outdone, managed to oppress and kill countless millions of people. Will the wonders of human pride and progressivism ever cease? All we have left to do is utterly cast off God's restraint and become "truly free." Imagine it! We're building a tower to the stars!

It is true that even though human beings are intrinsically fallible we're remarkable creatures with wide-ranging capabilities and spheres of interaction and enterprise. These can be categorized in numerous ways with names such as "spheres" or "mountains" of societal influence that are thought to mold the way everyone thinks and behaves and are identified as areas of human activity that are open to improvement.

Note the underlying observation that human nature and behavior are not only individually but systemically flawed and in ongoing need of correction and revision. How will reliably continuous personal and societal improvement of this broad scope ever happen? To make the task more visible, let's consider the generic and relatively inclusive outline of spheres presented in the following chart:

Kingdom: God's Reign in our Midst

†	Spheres of Human Life and Activity	Problems
1	Family Life – Marriage/Family Relationships, Reproduction, Child and Aged Care	Disruption
2	Religion – Ideology, Morality, Worship, Communal Rites/Rituals, Self-help	Falsehood
3	Education – Languages, Mathematics, Science, History, Study Skills, Trades	Ignorance
4	Government – Legislation, Criminal Justice, Politics, Protection, General Welfare	Oppression
5	Communication – Internet, Media, Language Interpretation, Radio/TV, Telephone	Confusion
6	Art and Music – Architecture, Design and Decoration, Fashion, Style	Contamination
7	Economics – Business, Commerce, Finance, Technology	Poverty/Greed
8	Human Services – Counseling, Medical Care, Social Services	Inequities
9	Agriculture – Food Production/Distribution, Nutrition, Dining	Hunger
10	Recreation – Entertainment, Hobbies, Sports	Idolatry
11	Infrastructure – Housing, Sanitation, Shipping, Transportation	Deterioration
12	Stewardship – Property, Land, Air and Water, Climate, Nature	Pollution

In recent years a somewhat controversial movement within the Christian community known as "dominion theology" has emerged which advocates for the transformation of society by focusing on redeeming a list of spheres similar to those outlined above prior to the Lord's return. Is this our future? Or, with all our human talent, will we keep forgetting God and making a mess of it?

Who will help us sort this all out and turn the ashes of our human failure into the fullness of our potential? The God of ages – Immanuel, our Creator, Redeemer, and Sustainer – is with us! And if God is with us who can stand against us? He will save, restore, guide, and support us with His grace, love, and wisdom. Our God is with us, Immanuel!

What a Wonderful World!

Kingdom: God's Reign in our Midst
E - His Kingdom, here now and forever

And it shall come to pass afterward, that I will pour out my Spirit on all flesh; your sons and your daughters shall prophesy, your old men shall dream dreams, and your young men shall see visions.   Joel 2:28 and Acts 2:17

Being asked by the Pharisees when the Kingdom of God would come, he answered them, "The Kingdom of God is not coming in ways that can be observed, nor will they say, 'Look, here it is!' or 'There!' for behold, the Kingdom of God is in the midst of you."   Luke 17:20-21

Universal Dreams of a Better World

Human beings are, by our very nature, creatures with dreams, hopes, and active imaginations. We carry within us an image of and a deep longing for an ideal that we all unconsciously compare with the reality of our lives. What is this ideal life and place that all of us desire and hope for, especially when we're uncomfortable or suffering?

1. A world with a better future for us and our family and community
2. A place where we and others do all things well, with care, love, kindness, understanding, simplicity, wisdom, virtue, beauty, peace, joy, prosperity, and harmony
3. A society where all needs are equitably met, people are satisfied with opportunities to grow and serve to their full capacity, to enjoy, appreciate and be appreciated, love and be loved
4. Literary examples: King Arthur's Camelot, Winthrop's biblical City Set on a Hill, Cosette's Castle on a Cloud, Dorothy's Somewhere Over the Rainbow, MLK's Beloved Community, the American Dream, the Kingdom of God, Paradise, Heaven.

On the other hand, we may find ourselves comparing our situation with something much worse: how closely does what we're going through now resemble "hell" on earth? My father served in the United States Army in combat for over 2 years during World War II. For a long time afterwards he wouldn't talk about his experience at all. Whenever one of us would ask, all he would say is "War is hell." Life can seem like that during times of tribulation such as severe economic depression, civil strife, grievous illness, horrendous loss, and terrorism.

Kingdom: God's Reign in our Midst

And then there are all the in-between times when things are "normal" – not perfect but far enough away from horrible to be OK. How do we sort out and make biblical sense of this spectrum of human experience and imagination, of our hopes and dreams, our fears and nightmares? Below is an outline made with four words derived from Greek: the two ends are well-known in literature and the middle two are usually used as clinical terms.

Utopia – ["no place"?] *The Kingdom of God on Earth*
An ideal world/society where everything works the way it should and people dwell together in harmony

Eutopia – ["a good place"] *Righteousness, meekness*
A condition in which an organ, organism, or organization is well positioned and operating the way it was designed to function

Ectopia – ["out of place"] *Sin (hamartia), unrighteousness*
A condition in which an organ, organism, or organization is not operating properly or is significantly out of order

Dystopia – ["a bad place"] *The absence of God on Earth*
A nightmare world/society where virtually everything is not working the way it should and people are in constant stress

From our faith tradition's point of view, these four overlapping realms may occur within the time and space of our universe, embedded in eternity by Heaven over the top; and Hell below the bottom.

When Jesus came as a man He revealed the "good news" that the Kingdom of God is emerging and accessible to us now in the midst of our lives together in community as well as within our own thought life and comprehension. He pointed back to the Law and the Prophets, the Scriptural record of God's faithfulness to mankind, and forward to a time in which God's justice and mercy will ultimately prevail through a Kingdom not made with human effort or imagination but conceived and established by God Himself. He encouraged us not to yearn for or become overly worried about earthly concerns but to

... seek first the Kingdom of God and his righteousness, and all these things will be added to you.   Matthew 6:33

Let's learn about His Kingdom and go up together, brothers and sisters, reach for the sky, look forward to our Lord coming on the clouds, and let go of every weight that holds us down. The best is yet to come!

Lesson 1E
Characteristics of kingdoms

Understanding 4: What is a kingdom? Understanding where we fit in the authority and social structures around us, including models of family, church, community, education, industry, and government.

Recognizing entities with definable "kingdom" authority structures, realms, and common understandings including behavioral guidelines, expectations, and sanctions.

Each one of us has an idea that comes to mind when we think of a kingdom. We might imagine the big round table surrounded by brave knights in King Arthur's court in the mythological Kingdom of Logres with its utopian castle city of Camelot, giants, dragons, magicians, and loyal citizens. More likely we'll think of historical kings and queens in past empires and nations around the world or the remnants of these that remain in today's world, most of which have been superseded by modern democracies.

Surely, we think, we're beyond the outdated concepts of being part of a kingdom or actually ruled by a king in this enlightened age, since most of the ones that remain are just ceremonial remnants of a dead and dying way of governing. One carryover might be the centuries-old concept expressed in the British proverb that "a man's home is his castle," first articulated in 1604 in a legal decision by Sir Edward Coke. Later Coke included it in his 4-volume *Institutes of the Lawes of England* which was profoundly influential in establishing common law within the British Empire and its colonies.

The concept behind Coke's folksy proverb is that a family home with its activities, grounds, and possessions is an orderly and protected space where a husband can watch over, provide for, and guard his family from unwelcome intrusion. Coke's idea clearly identifies the common characteristics of kingdoms: an authority (the head of the house or "*king*"), a mutually understood set of functions, and a domain of influence (the "*dom*") within which the king's authority is exercised.

Kingdom: God's Reign in our Midst

Since the advent of the Internet, the word *domain* has become quite modern in identifying addresses (called URLs or Uniform Resource Locators) on the Web that various groups have obtained exclusive authority over to develop and maintain their activities.

Simply put a kingdom is a definable realm or domain over which an identifiable person has authority, whether that is a home, an Internet address, an organized business, or a governmental entity. Seen in this light, there are basically two kinds of kingdoms: temporal and eternal. Temporal or worldly kingdoms invariably come and go, since they are limited in time and space. In contrast, the everlasting Kingdom of God transcends both time and space.

In addition to its domain being unlimited by time and space, there is another characteristic that is unique to the Kingdom of God, the way in which authority is usually exercised within it. The last lesson in the previous study in this series on Awakening noted the distinction between top-down and bottom-up authority:

Pyramids of The World

(CEO / Top mgt / Middle mgt / Supervisory cadre / Working category)

World's systems: Its bosses exercise top down authority and you work for them.

God's Kingdom: Our King gave his life for us and we serve one another as family.

Tree of Life in God's Kingdom

As Jesus told His disciples shortly before the Last Supper and His crucifixion,

"You know that the rulers of the Gentiles lord it over them, and their great ones exercise authority over them. It shall not be so among you. But whoever would be great among you must be your servant, and whoever would be first among you must be your slave, even as the Son of Man came not to be served but to serve, and to give his life as a ransom for many." Matthew 20:25-28

Using the broader definition of "kingdom" we've been examining, let's take a personal inventory by looking at some of the entities in our modern world that would qualify as kingdoms. Begin by applying Edward Coke's definition to your home. What kind of authority is being exercised there? Is your home a worldly kingdom or one that is becoming infused with God's Kingdom authority? Going further, how about your school or workplace? Are your daily activities under the authority of a boss or director or guided by servant leadership? Consider your faith community: how is your local assembly or the national organization or denomination to which it belongs organized? What about the government in your local area, state, and nation? In the United States we have an interesting historical seal on our dollar bills:

Note that the shining eye overseeing the pyramid depicts the new 3-branch form of top-down authority our nation's founders developed (the *novus ordo seclorum* or "new order of the ages") to replace the solitary emperor, king, or pharaoh of human monarchy with an elite system that might attract more providential favor (*annuit coeptis*).

Recognizing that no human system is perfectly good or evil, how are we doing, personally and corporately? Let's spend some time together evaluating the "kingdoms" that are impacting our lives.

The authority structures in my life

1. What was your home life like while you were growing up? Was it orderly, safe and predictable? How was authority exercised?

2. What about your home life now? Who is "in charge" and how is their authority being carried out and received?

Kingdom: God's Reign in our Midst

14

3. What have your experiences been like with schools and jobs? What kind of "kingdoms" have your teachers and employers established?

4. How are business, criminal justice, and governmental affairs being handled in your local area? How godly or worldly are they?

5. What about the affairs of your state and nation? Are developments and relationships in these "kingdoms" moving in godly directions?

Be thoughtful in responding to each question. You might appreciate reviewing our online handout on **A Confession of Dependence** at www.celebratesalvation.org/more/#2.

Lesson 2E
Worldly kingdoms

Understanding 4: What is a kingdom? Understanding where we fit in the authority and social structures around us, including models of family, church, community, education, industry, and government.

Observing the multiple overlapping forms of worldly structure that organize our communal activities in business, education, entertainment, family, governance, and religion.

Somehow the human activities of our world need to be organized and carried out with a measure of efficiency and oversight for our lives to be sustained and prosper. We have ongoing needs for air, water, food, shelter, training, jobs, and protection. How can we work together in the diverse society that surrounds us as we seek to have our needs met?

Over the millennia various ways have been developed. The Bible and anthropology agree that we were hunter-gatherers who learned early on how to cultivate the earth and raise animals. Along the way we banded together for mutual support, built shelters, and "became civilized." It probably happened somewhat naturally, the way birds learn how to eat and fly and build nests. The stronger and more successful ones lived, and the weaker ones didn't last as long and eventually died out. Darwin wasn't the only one who saw it.

Might and power, cleverness and communication, pride and prejudice, winning friends and influencing people. As Brer Rabbit would say, "Some goes up and some goes down, that's what makes the world go round." Does any of this sound a bit cynical? Well, that's simply recognizing that playing king of the mountain, empire building, and jockeying for position are part of our fallen human nature.

So how did we civilize this process? We developed organized human structures with goals, directions and purposes, principles and values, authority and leadership, and even ideologies, mythologies, and stories to hold them together. We formed into tribes, bands, cooperatives,

Kingdom: God's Reign in our Midst

businesses, schools, cultural and religious organizations, governments, and performing troops of all description. Each outfit has at least one purpose and a structured way of going about carrying it out. Someone is in charge with others who report to them. Below these are managers of various aspects and under their oversight are the workers who carry out all the associated tasks. When put on a chart, it's always pyramidal.

Governance for establishing submission to behavioral boundaries and community norms can come in a number of forms from dictatorships like absolute empires and monarchies to various more representative forms. An executive leader may be supported by a board or cabinet of advisors. Checks and balances may be set up as offsets for human error and greed for wealth and power. Somehow, by God's grace, it all holds together for a while, sometimes for better, other times for worse.

Let's step back for a moment and recognize who is doing all this – fallible human beings. We start out as helpless, uneducated, innocent babies and slowly develop into somewhat more helpful, educated, and less innocent adults. As we mature we try to learn and pass on what we've learned to others. Then we die. Is it any wonder that the world is mixed up and needs more insight, wisdom, and understanding?

Where, in the midst of life's toils and tribulations, will we be able to get the help we need other than from people who are just as broken and incomplete as we are? Jesus has the answer:

All things have been handed over to me by my Father, and no one knows the Son except the Father, and no one knows the Father except the Son and anyone to whom the Son chooses to reveal him. Come to me, all who labor and are heavy laden, and I will give you rest. Take my yoke upon you, and learn from me, for I am gentle and lowly in heart, and you will find rest for your souls. For my yoke is easy, and my burden is light." Matthew 11:27-30

This is very good news that becomes better and better as people believe and take hold of it. The process outlined by Jesus in this revelation of His divine love are: 1) Recognizing our burden, 2) Coming to Him for help, 3) Taking His yoke upon us, 4) Learning from Him, and 5) Finding and entering into His rest. There are problems with each step. We have a hard time admitting we need help and trusting someone we don't know very well yet to provide it. Then, once we've discovered that the One making the offer is the loving King of the Universe and have gotten past these two hang-ups, we discover that there's a catch to taking His yoke upon us. We have to sell out to really get the whole package!

The kingdom of heaven is like a merchant in search of fine pearls, who, on finding one pearl of great value, went and sold all that he had and bought it.

Matthew 13:45-46

The transition we've arrived at is from looking at the kingdoms of this world from within them to moving out of the world into the place of eternity where Jesus rules and reigns. We can then see these worldly kingdoms from His perspective and receive His wisdom. Please understand that a measure of wisdom is available to all, but without being intentional and wholehearted we stand to lose our grip on whatever might be offered to us.

If any of you lacks wisdom, let him ask God, who gives generously to all without reproach, and it will be given him. But let him ask in faith, with no doubting, for the one who doubts is like a wave of the sea that is driven and tossed by the wind. For that person must not suppose that he will receive anything from the Lord; he is a double-minded man, unstable in all his ways.

James 1:5-8

The worldly kingdoms in my life

1. What are the large and small worldly "kingdoms" that overlap in your life (see Page 8)? List as many of them as you can below.

2. Using our **Organization diagram drawing** handout*, try making a rough organizational diagram of each "kingdom" you've listed above, labelling it with notes and answers to the following: Who is in charge? Where do you fit into "line of command"?

Kingdom: God's Reign in our Midst

3. Note below some issues you might be having in each "kingdom." Where could you use some help? Have you asked God?

4. What ideas do you have about improving what is being done in any of these "kingdoms"? How can you go about offering your insights?

5. How do you handle the frustrations you have to deal with in the world's systems that impact your life? Where do you go with them?

* Go online to www.celebratesalvation.org/more/#2 and print out copies of our handout **Organization diagram drawing** template to answer Question 2 on the previous page. Also: if you aren't familiar with the Serenity Prayer on Page 6, take a little time now to review it.

Lesson 3E
The Kingdom of God

Understanding 4: What is a kingdom? Understanding where we fit in the authority and social structures around us, including models of family, church, community, education, industry, and government.

Visualizing the all-encompassing rule and reign of the triune God of our faith in the universe and the affairs of mankind throughout space, time, and eternity.

So far we've spent some time looking at the various kinds of kingdoms, large and small, that we find ourselves living and working within. We've noted some of the differences between the basic authority structure of the kingdoms of this world and the Kingdom of our God and our need for wisdom in dealing with them.

But what about the Kingdom of God itself, apart from the kingdoms of this world. Can they be distinguished from each other, and if so how? Here's a list of more aspects of God's Kingdom to contemplate:

1. Since God dwells in eternity and created time itself, He is able to observe and rule His Kingdom from "a place" that's beyond time and yet touches it at every point. Time and space are not limits.

2. When God initiated the "Big Bang" recorded in Genesis 1 He created not only light but time, space, and matter and set them in motion. Current estimates calculate that the observable Universe is about 150 *billion* light-years across. God is in the midst of this vast Universe, ruling and reigning over a virtually limitless domain.

3. An incredibly intricate set of mathematical, material, chemical, and spiritual laws and interrelationships holds us and our Universe together. Who other than God could possibly design, create, control, and keep track of them all?

4. And then we come to the apex of Creation – life and people. The entire enterprise is so vast that it's virtually incomprehensible. How does God govern all of life, especially those of us with free will?

Kingdom: God's Reign in our Midst

As you ponder these observations, you might want to start an Internet tour here: https://hiskingdom.us/alpha/creation. Shall we just say it? The Kingdom of God constitutes an entirely unique realm. To compare it with the worldly kingdoms we've put together here on earth using our human talents, time, and treasure is almost blasphemous. And yet our God sent His only begotten Son into our world as a baby:

Christ Jesus, who, though he was in the form of God, did not count equality with God a thing to be grasped, but emptied himself, by taking the form of a servant, being born in the likeness of men. And being found in human form, he humbled himself by becoming obedient to the point of death, even death on a cross. Therefore God has highly exalted him and bestowed on him the name that is above every name, so that at the name of Jesus every knee should bow, in heaven and on earth and under the earth, and every tongue confess that Jesus Christ is Lord, to the glory of God the Father. Philippians 2:5-11

This is our King in the midst of His domain, exercising his servant authority on our behalf in love and obedience. How can we do anything but bow down and worship Him, the God of the Universe, the King of Kings and Lord of Lords?

There are over 100 references in the New Testament to Jesus talking about the Kingdom. Where can we start? It's probably best just to look at the material universe of time, light, and matter with awe and wonder and leave its management up to God (unless, of course, we've been involved in messing it up). We can study time and space scientifically, theoretically, and technologically and never come to an end This part of God and His creation is absolutely amazing! As Paul wrote:

For his invisible attributes, namely, his eternal power and divine nature, have been clearly perceived, ever since the creation of the world, in the things that have been made. Romans 1:20

But if this isn't enough to "blow our minds" all we have to do is turn our attention to the condition of humanity. Speaking of things we've been involved in messing up, here's a prime example. We can't even govern ourselves, much less the entire kaleidoscopic world of fallible human beings. Love and hate, war and peace, crime and punishment, wealth and poverty, power and prestige, truth and falsehood, jealousy and covetousness… how would you like to have the job? No thanks, you can be the King, Jesus, but I'd like to be your helper.

What keeps us from getting our lives synchronized with His? Primarily two things: commitment and competition, priority and perseverance.

You shall love the Lord your God with all your heart and with all your soul and with all your mind. This is the great and first commandment. And a second is like it: You shall love your neighbor as yourself. On these two commandments depend all the Law and the Prophets. Matthew 22:37-40

We divide our time with the world and all its distractions, lose our focus, and the seed falls on rocky ground as Jesus noted in His parable about the sower and the seed. His key underlying instruction is:

Therefore I tell you, do not be anxious about your life… But seek first the Kingdom of God and his righteousness, and all these things will be added to you. Matthew 6:25-33

If grasping what God's Kingdom is about continues to be a challenging topic for you, please remember what Jesus told Nicodemus:

Truly, truly, I say to you, unless one is born again he cannot see the Kingdom of God. John 3:3

Awakening to the reality of God's Kingdom

1. Have you entrusted your life entirely to your Creator, the King of Kings? If not, what do you think might be holding you back?

2. When do you think the Kingdom of God started and when do you think it will come to an end?

Kingdom: God's Reign in our Midst

22

3. When was the last time you reviewed the parables Jesus taught about the Kingdom of God? Are any confusing to you?

4. Do you think it's possible to know how to carry out the second great commandment without being devoted to the first?

5. What questions about the Kingdom of God are in your mind right now? Make a list below and come back to it often.

Our handout on **12 Parables about the Kingdom of God** (available at www.celebratesalvation.org/more/#2) can be a very helpful resource. While you're in this Lesson, don't miss the opportunity to affirm and confirm your salvation, rebirth, and adoption as a child of God.

Lesson 4E
Being *in* or *of* a kingdom

Understanding 4: What is a kingdom? Understanding where we fit in the authority and social structures around us, including models of family, church, community, education, industry, and government.

Assessing our relationships with the kingdoms of mankind and the Kingdom of God in terms of our personal commitment, identity, and time invested.

"They are not of the world, just as I am not of the world."   John 17:16

Who are we, and where do we belong? How much of what we're involved in defines our core identity? These are central questions of being and self-image that we're all called to address seriously. Initially our sense of personal identity comes from our families of origin. Our genetic sex is usually recognized at birth and then confirmed as gender by those around us through word choice and customary patterns of dress and behavior. Our given names often reflect our gender and family identities as well. We learn language and inherit culture.

Racial and ethnic identities develop along with extended family heritage and special interests and talents. We might become known as a "shy black girl who likes science" or an "outgoing Hispanic boy who is good at sports." Regional and national elements enter in as we grow older: we're rural or urban, from the North or South, American or French.

Then puberty, adolescence, and emerging adulthood arrive. Where do I fit into this big world with all of my hopes, dreams, and issues? Will I be an artist or a factory worker, a housewife or a race car driver, a doctor or a gang member? Am I loveable or too messed up to be loved? How do I handle my failings and feelings? Who Am I??

There are lots of places we can find identities to try on: schools, jobs, churches, social groups, and a host of personal relationships. We might be attracted to a religious group by the nice people there, so we spend some years in their midst but get hurt and start seeing the hypocrisy. The local yacht club is a nice way to mingle with prosperous people and get out on the water in style, too. My job has promoted me, and I think I really belong here: I could make this company my career. I'd like to be known by the sporty car I drive, so I wear stuff with its logo on it. It was a lot of work, but finally I got my doctorate! I fit in! Fill in the blank:

I am a _____.

What we're talking about is how much our personal identities are wrapped up in the commitments, relationships, and time we invest in the world around us. Until we come into a personal relationship with the living God, all of these are primarily fleshly and worldly. In a very real way, we're children of the earth and offspring of Adam. We belong to one or more of the Babylonian companies, Egyptian armies, or sectarian parties of our world. To be otherwise would be impossible, given our human heritage and circumstances.

What about the Kingdom of God (or Heaven)? First a simple statement of fact: the visible "church" is not the Kingdom of God. It's a mixed gathering of people who have expressed varying levels of interest in spiritual matters, a worldly "holding area" so to speak. The "church" hopefully contains many who have gone through the Door which Jesus opened and become committed Kingdom citizens, but not everyone there is "in the Kingdom." Many are simply curious, poorly informed, or uncommitted. As Jesus revealed in His Sermon on the Mount:

Again, the kingdom of heaven is like a net that was thrown into the sea and gathered fish of every kind. When it was full, men drew it ashore and sat down and sorted the good into containers but threw away the bad. So it will be at the end of the age. The angels will come out and separate the evil from the righteous and throw them into the fiery furnace. In that place there will be weeping and gnashing of teeth.   Matthew 13:47-52

Jesus tells a similar story in Matthew 13:24-43 when the similar-appearing "tares" (weeds) are separated from the true wheat at the end of the age. The only way to be enrolled as a fellow-citizen in the Kingdom of God is to accept the offer made to us by God at His own costly expense to become His child as an adopted sibling of Jesus:

Enter by the narrow gate. For the gate is wide and the way is easy that leads to destruction, and those who enter by it are many.   Matthew 7:13

Understanding 4   Lesson 4E

Then Jesus told his disciples, "If anyone would come after me, let him deny himself and take up his cross and follow me. Matthew 16:24

The "church" is called to be an embassy of the Kingdom of God, but there is literally no other way to enter but through the blood of Jesus.

The kingdom of heaven is like treasure hidden in a field, which a man found and covered up. Then in his joy he goes and sells all that he has and buys that field... For where your treasure is, there your heart will be also.

Matthew 13:44; 6:21

We may have several problems with God's plan, however. We don't know enough about it or what we know is wrong. The price is too high. We prefer the "*old wine*" of our religion to the "*new wine*" of God's gift. We don't really believe that God cares that much about our small lives. We think most Christians are just a bunch of stuck-up hypocrites. In short, we have too many clever rationalizations for our own good.

Are you ready to do a personal assessment of how you're relating to the world's kingdoms and God's Kingdom? Lets' give it a go!

Finding out where you fit

1. What are the sources of your personal identity? List them below, and then number them in order of importance to you.

2. To what extent do you believe your participation or role in any of your significant organized groups determines who you are?

Kingdom: God's Reign in our Midst

26

3. What does being "born again" mean to you? Are you growing as an adopted child of God? If not, what is holding you back?

4. Can someone be an active member in a worldly group while staying true to their primary allegiance to God's Kingdom? Are you?

5. Are there areas of your life and involvements that make you feel uncomfortable or that you think you should change? List them.

If you are unsure about whether you are truly part of God's Kingdom as an adopted child of God, please pray and seek counsel from solid believers you can trust. *"I write these things to you who believe in the name of the Son of God, that you may know that you have eternal life."* 1 John 5:13

Lesson 5E
Establishing our priorities

Understanding 5: Our dual citizenship: How to live fruitful lives simultaneously in the temporal kingdoms of this world and the everlasting Kingdom of God.

What it means to "seek first the Kingdom of God and His righteousness" and then maintain that priority consistently.

What do you think of when the word "priorities" comes up? A list of things to be done? An orderly list of what's important to you? A tally of deadlines and expectations? Oughts and shoulds? All of the above? Priorities are simply a way of sorting out how much of ourselves we're willing to invest in the variety of activities and commitments that we're facing. Establishing our priorities then involves assessing both our available time and our personal involvements: how much time and effort are we willing to spend on each area and when will we do it?

Actually, our lives are pretty full as it is, and often we find ourselves living from day to day or even moment to moment. We fall prey to the "tyranny of the urgent" by just hopping on the "rat race" treadmill every day and doing one pressing thing after another. Isn't that what Jesus meant in His Sermon on the Mount when He said, "*Therefore do not be anxious about tomorrow, for tomorrow will be anxious for itself. Sufficient for the day is its own trouble.*"? No, this verse has to do with anxiety and worry, not prayerful priority-setting.

The first step in establishing priorities is getting a good fix on who you are (identity), where you are (physical, organizational, and social location), what you've been equipped to do (your gifts and talents), and how you're being called to fit into God's plan right now. Along the way we each face a lot of competition for our time and energy, much of which is either a distraction, things that may appear to be good but actually compete with God's best, or wasteful and downright ungodly things that head us in wrong directions. Solomon described the situation many of us find ourselves in when he wrote the following (see Page 55 for my personal expanded translation of this verse):

Kingdom: God's Reign in our Midst

Where there is no prophetic vision the people cast off restraint, but blessed is he who keeps the law.   Proverbs 29:18

Hmm. That's funny. I thought that proverb had to do with big spooky visions of "Thus sayeth the Lord" and stuff like that. What it really has to do with is looking prayerfully into the future while seeking God's guidance, comparing what we sense is coming up in the way of tasks and opportunities, and carefully synchronizing our lives with God's plans for us. The opposite of "casting off restraint" is being sensitive and disciplined. The opposite of "keeping the law" is doing our own thing. The person who won't look ahead will find themselves making one avoidable mistake after another.

How do we get God's guidance? Proverbs 3:5-8 gives us the key:

Trust in the Lord with all your heart, and do not lean on your own understanding. In all your ways acknowledge him, and he will make straight your paths. Be not wise in your own eyes; fear the Lord, and turn away from evil. It will be healing to your flesh and refreshment to your bones.

But how do we hear God's voice and get His wisdom?

If any of you lacks wisdom, let him ask God, who gives generously to all without reproach, and it will be given him.   James 1:5

OK, now we are getting closer to the question of how we establish our priorities on the Rock. Jesus' foundational Word will guide us:

"You shall love the Lord your God with all your heart and with all your soul and with all your mind. This is the great and first commandment. And a second is like it: You shall love your neighbor as yourself. On these two commandments depend all the Law and the Prophets."   Matthew 22:37-40

"Therefore do not be anxious, saying, 'What shall we eat?' or 'What shall we drink?' or 'What shall we wear?' For the Gentiles seek after all these things, and your heavenly Father knows that you need them all. But seek first the Kingdom of God and his righteousness, and all these things will be added to you."   Matthew 6:31-33

There's our answer! Our first priority is always to love God and seek Him and His Kingdom first in all we do. This, of course involves discernment to distinguish between God's will and the ever-present temptations of our flesh, deceptions of our spiritual enemies, and distractions of this fallen world. With commitment, prayer, knowledge of the Scriptures, appropriate consultation with others, and practice, God's will becomes both easier to grasp and carry out. And the result becomes filled with the wonderful fruit of the Spirit for all to enjoy!

Now what we want to do is develop the habit of living in God's love and Word, of enjoying His Kingdom and His righteousness, of abiding in the Vine as Jesus exhorted us. And the key to developing a habit is the same for musicians, doctors, and everyone: practice, practice, practice! With His guidance and support, practice makes perfect and its discipline matures us into His disciples.

Abide in me, and I in you. As the branch cannot bear fruit by itself, unless it abides in the vine, neither can you, unless you abide in me. I am the vine; you are the branches. Whoever abides in me and I in him, he it is that bears much fruit, for apart from me you can do nothing.   John 15:4-5

Letting God establish our daily priorities

1. What do you imagine when you ask the Lord for His Kingdom to come and His will to be done "on earth as it is in heaven"?

2. Do any of the petitions offered in the Lord's Prayer pertain to you personally? Which ones, and how?

30

3. What does the term "His righteousness" mean to you? How are you actively seeking it?

4. How do you think you could concentrate your efforts more on "seeking the Kingdom of God and His righteousness"?

5. Examine the priorities in your life closely and make a list below indicating where you want to ask God to help you improve.

A prayer for discernment: *Father, please quicken the gift of discernment in me by the power and presence of your Holy Spirit to guide my thoughts, actions, and priorities according to Your will for my life. Show me how to seek Your Kingdom and Your righteousness as I live my life in the light of your love.*

Lesson 6E
Qualitative differences

Understanding 5: Our dual citizenship: How to live fruitful lives simultaneously in the temporal kingdoms of this world and the everlasting Kingdom of God.

Distinguishing between situations where cooperation with a worldly kingdom can be sustained and where becoming "unequally yoked" is a serious risk.

Let's examine a passage in 2 Corinthians, remembering as we do what Peter wrote about Paul's epistles in 2 Peter 3:16 when he warned,

There are some things in them that are hard to understand, which the ignorant and unstable twist to their own destruction, as they do the other Scriptures.

Now for the difficult passage:

Do not be unequally yoked with unbelievers. For what partnership has righteousness with lawlessness? Or what fellowship has light with darkness? What accord has Christ with Belial? Or what portion does a believer share with an unbeliever? What agreement has the temple of God with idols? For we are the temple of the living God; as God said, "I will make my dwelling among them and walk among them, and I will be their God, and they shall be my people. Therefore go out from their midst, and be separate from them, says the Lord, and touch no unclean thing; then I will welcome you, and I will be a father to you, and you shall be sons and daughters to me, says the Lord Almighty."

2 Corinthians 6:14-18

Scripture is not saying that we, as believers, should not associate with unbelievers or people who don't agree with us. Where would we live and work and engage in commerce? How and with whom would we be able to grow in faith and share the Gospel message? As Paul indicated in 1 Corinthians 5:9-11,

I wrote to you in my letter not to associate with sexually immoral people – not at all meaning the sexually immoral of this world, or the greedy and swindlers, or idolaters, since then you would need to go out of the world… but not to associate with anyone who bears the name of brother if he is guilty of sexual immorality or

Kingdom: God's Reign in our Midst

greed, or is an idolater, reviler, drunkard, or swindler – not even to eat with such a one."

This is strong but clear language. Following up in 1 Corinthians 6:11, Paul notes that we were once separated from God as unbelievers also, *"but you were washed, you were sanctified, you were justified in the name of the Lord Jesus Christ and by the Spirit of our God."* Again in Romans 5:8 Paul reminds us that *"God shows his love for us in that while we were still sinners, Christ died for us."*

Jesus Himself associated with sinners and developed a bad reputation among some of the religious leaders in the community for doing so. What Scripture is warning us about is being *"unequally yoked"* with those whose beliefs and lifestyles are at odds with ours which begs the question of how we are "yoked" now. Jesus illuminated the question when He invited us in Matthew 11:28-30 to trade in our current heavy "yoke" for His relatively light and easy one:

> *Come to me, all who labor and are heavy laden, and I will give you rest. Take my yoke upon you, and learn from me, for I am gentle and lowly in heart, and you will find rest for your souls. For my yoke is easy, and my burden is light."*

Once we've been set free in Christ from the world's heavy yokes we're encouraged to learn from Him and avoid going back to our old ways of thinking and relating. As Paul put it in his letter to the Galatians, *"For freedom Christ has set us free; stand firm therefore, and do not submit again to a yoke of slavery."* Simply stated, being "unequally yoked" will entangle and enslave us again with the burdens, cares and concerns of this world.

Perhaps one of the most obvious ways to be unequally yoked together with a person is by becoming married to an unbeliever. Often times this happens by falsely equating *eros* or fleshly romantic love with *agape* or divinely inspired love. Fruitful and joyful marriage calls for a deep spiritual bond that is confirmed and sealed with *agape* love.

Another common example would be entering into a legal business partnership with an unbeliever. Business dealings often involve ethical and moral decisions about truthfulness, honesty, and integrity. Partners need to "see eye to eye" and share common goals and values. Without this kind of agreement, believers may find themselves in costly, painful, and wasteful disagreements that can end in serious compromise or even legal separation and divorce.

What other kinds of unequally yoked situations could we find ourselves in, and which ones might be safely entered into with care? Let's consider the following realms as examples: personal life, business, politics, and social activism. Here's a warning in 1 Corinthians 6:18:

Flee from sexual immorality. Every other sin a person commits is outside the body, but the sexually immoral person sins against his own body.

Avoid working for or with a corporate entity that holds values that are at odds with your conscience whenever possible. Political parties, campaigning for candidates, and social activist causes are all potentially questionable activities that should only be entered into with caution and prayer for guidance. And as "soldiers" in the Kingdom of God, we will always do well to heed the counsel Paul gave in 2 Timothy 2:4:

No soldier gets entangled in civilian pursuits, since his aim is to please the one who enlisted him.

My participation in the world as a believer

1. How clearly are you able to distinguish between your Kingdom identity and commitments and your worldly involvements?

2. Do you think you may be "unequally yoked" in any of your activities or relationships? If so, list them below with brief notes.

3. What is your current job or employment situation like? Can you identify any difficulties with your Christian commitments there?

4. Are you involved in any political or social action causes? Have any of them negatively affected your emotional state or relationships?

5. What activities are you currently engaged in that you're wondering about right now? How might you clarify your involvements there?

You may appreciate reading our **Divine Obsession** handout, available at www.celebratesalvation.org/more/#2, for greater insight into and evaluation of your underlying attitude toward social action as a believer.

Lesson 7E
Awareness of our standing

Understanding 5: Our dual citizenship: How to live fruitful lives simultaneously in the temporal kingdoms of this world and the everlasting Kingdom of God.

Being as "wise as serpents and innocent as doves" in our social interactions without compromising our primary commitment to God's Kingdom and righteousness.

Given our forgetful human nature, one question we have to ask ourselves over and over is, "Where am I standing." Back in 1834 in the midst of his vital pulpit and hymn-writing ministry, Edward Mote penned the following timeless lyrics drawn from Jesus' Parable of the Wise and the Foolish Builders in Matthew 7:24-27 and Luke 6:46-49:

> *My hope is built on nothing less than Jesus' blood and righteousness.*
> *I dare not trust the sweetest frame but wholly lean on Jesus' name.*
> *On Christ the solid rock I stand. All other ground is sinking sand.*

We have become members of the "church" (*ekklesia*) by being called out of the world, adopted into God's family by the power of the Holy Spirit though the sacrifice of Jesus, and returned to the world as Kingdom ambassadors. Although our lives are being carried out "in the world" again, we are "of the Kingdom" now and the "house" we're living in the midst of has been "built upon the Rock" of Christ, the Word made flesh. Here's a challenging exhortation from Paul:

> *Now this I say and testify in the Lord, that you must no longer walk as the Gentiles do, in the futility of their minds. They are darkened in their understanding, alienated from the life of God because of the ignorance that is in them, due to their hardness of heart... But that is not the way you learned Christ! – assuming that you have heard about him and were taught in him, as the truth is in Jesus, to put off your old self, which belongs to your former manner of life and is corrupt through deceitful desires, and to be renewed in the spirit of your minds, and to put on the new self, created after the likeness of God in true righteousness and holiness.* Ephesians 4:17-24

Kingdom: God's Reign in our Midst

The "Gentiles" Paul is referring to are the people of the world, among whom we all once walked in relative harmony before we were spiritually awakened to God's love and life. Now, however, we have to keep remembering our true identities, first and foremost, as "*new creatures in Christ*" and "*children of God*" our Father.

What does this involve? Following up on the guidance we've just reviewed in Ephesians 4, we need to center our lives in the spiritual realm by being aware of what's going on in our hearts and minds:

Take every thought captive to obey Christ.

2 Corinthians 10:5

Ask, and it will be given to you; seek, and you will find; knock, and it will be opened to you.

Matthew 7:7

Trust in the Lord with all your heart, and do not lean on your own understanding. In all your ways acknowledge him, and he will make straight your paths.

Proverbs 3:5-6

We need to be present and stay focused in all of our relationships, first with our Lord and Savior and then with those we're with at the time, in other words our neighbors. Why? Because there are always so many troublesome distractions right there to mislead us and trip us up as soon as our mental and spiritual "sobriety and vigilance" lapses. Where do these influences that distract us from our identity and purpose in Christ come from? Traditionally they've been identified as the world, the flesh, and the devil. Let's look at each one more closely.

1. **The World:** This source comes from the society around us through media, current issues and events, unexamined advice and input from colleagues and friends, and the often unspoken rules of the culture in which we live.

2. **The Flesh:** The urges and desires of our own human nature for acceptance, comfort, nurture, power, prestige, relief from stress, sexual gratification, social position, and wealth.

3. **The Devil:** Distracting and intrusive thoughts about ourselves and others and what's happening in the world around us. These can be personal or more pervasive notions about how things work in the world coming from the fallen spiritual powers and principalities that constitute the so-called *zeitgeist* or "spirit of the age."

In this mix, where does participation in church, community, and political activities come in? The author of Hebrews and Paul in his Epistle to the Ephesians lay out an applicable version of the two Great Commandments, to love God and our neighbor as ourselves:

Let us draw near [to God] with a true heart in full assurance of faith, with our hearts sprinkled clean from an evil conscience and our bodies washed with pure water. Let us hold fast the confession of our hope without wavering, for he who promised is faithful. And let us consider how to stir up one another [those around us] to love and good works, not neglecting to meet together [with other believers], as is the habit of some, but encouraging one another, and all the more as you see the Day drawing near… Therefore take up the whole armor of God, that you may be able to withstand in the evil day, and having done all, to stand firm.

Hebrews 10:22-25 and Ephesians 6:13

This leaves participation in the ongoing drama of civil government unaddressed, a subject we will be investigating in Lesson 8.

Standing on God's wisdom in a fallen world

1. Where do you see the boundary lines between the call of God's Kingdom and your involvement in the affairs of the world?

2. How do you feel that the world's concerns may have overtaken your vision for and commitment to His Kingdom and His ways?

38

3. What are some steps you could take to become more discerning and committed in carrying out God's will in your life?

4. Are there any specific distractions in your personal, home, or work life that you might be able to refocus and overcome?

5. Can you tell when you're getting off track? Give some examples of when you've been able to "take your thoughts captive" and refocus.

Read our **Forbidden Fruit** handout for greater understanding of His spiritual discernment plan, and consider reviewing your devotional life by using our **Reset Daily Devotional Plan** handout, available in Book 1 Resources at www.celebratesalvation.org/more.

Lesson 8E
Maintaining integrity

Understanding 5: Our dual citizenship: How to live fruitful lives simultaneously in the temporal kingdoms of this world and the everlasting Kingdom of God.

Growing in knowledge and understanding of God's will and being consistent in how we "Render to Caesar the things that are Caesar's and to God the things that are God's."

And they came and said to him, "Teacher, we know that you are true and do not care about anyone's opinion. For you are not swayed by appearances, but truly teach the way of God. Is it lawful to pay taxes to Caesar, or not? Should we pay them, or should we not?" But, knowing their hypocrisy, he said to them, "Why put me to the test? Bring me a denarius and let me look at it." And they brought one. And he said to them, "Whose likeness and inscription is this?" They said to him, "Caesar's." Jesus said to them, "Render to Caesar the things that are Caesar's, and to God the things that are God's." And they marveled at him.

Mark 12:13-17

On the face of it, this seems pretty straightforward. By now we should have a growing appreciation for who "God" is, but do we know who "Caesar" is in our lives? When Jesus spoke these words, Caesar was the title of the leader of the pagan Roman Empire that had overtaken the local government of Israel and its senate, the Sanhedrin. This made Caesar the head of the civil authority that ruled the people of Israel and Palestine. What else does God's Word say about civil authority?

Let every person be subject to the governing authorities. For there is no authority except from God, and those that exist have been instituted by God. Therefore whoever resists the authorities resists what God has appointed, and those who resist will incur judgment.
Romans 13:1-2

Be subject for the Lord's sake to every human institution, whether it be to the emperor as supreme, or to governors as sent by him to punish those who do evil and to praise those who do good. For this is the will of God, that by doing good you should put to silence the ignorance of foolish people.
1 Peter 2:13-15

Kingdom: God's Reign in our Midst

Suffice it to say at this point that the Kingdom of God and civil authority are two different structures, both under God's oversight. When human beings have blended the two, as they did when Israel asked Samuel to appoint a king over them (see 1 Samuel 8) and when the early church was absorbed into the Roman Empire under Constantine, both civil government and the Kingdom of God suffer.

No, there is only one Kingdom of God but a host of civil governments, some in better shape than others. As Psalm 2 notes, the world and its rulers are a mess. People are coming and going every which way, and the media are in a constant tizzy. The strife, violence, sex, political divisions, and economic gyrations of our modern world provide a perpetual mental Mixmaster that seems designed to keep us stirred up.

How close to representing the Kingdom are the governments of China, Russia, India, Iraq, Syria, Israel, Egypt, France, Germany, England, Mexico, Venezuela, or the United States, to name several? Before we lament, let's ask ourselves, "How close to representing the Kingdom is Babylon supposed to be?" and then "What does God expect of us?"

> *Thus says the Lord of hosts, the God of Israel, to all the exiles whom I have sent into exile from Jerusalem to Babylon: Build houses and live in them; plant gardens and eat their produce. Take wives and have sons and daughters; take wives for your sons, and give your daughters in marriage, that they may bear sons and daughters; multiply there, and do not decrease. But seek the welfare of the city where I have sent you into exile, and pray to the Lord on its behalf, for in its welfare you will find your welfare.* Jeremiah 29:4-7

Babylon is not our home, and the "American Dream" is not our dream.

> *But you are a chosen race, a royal priesthood, a holy nation, a people for his own possession, that you may proclaim the excellencies of him who called you out of darkness into his marvelous light. Once you were not a people, but now you are God's people; once you had not received mercy, but now you have received mercy. Beloved, I urge you as sojourners and exiles to abstain from the passions of the flesh, which wage war against your soul. Keep your conduct among the Gentiles honorable, so that when they speak against you as evildoers, they may see your good deeds and glorify God on the day of visitation.* 1 Peter 2:9-12

As Jeremiah and Peter have noted, we are "*sojourners and exiles*" whose true home is with God in His Kingdom. Once we understand this, maintaining our identities as children of God and ambassadors of Christ while acting as responsible citizens in the worldly kingdoms where we live becomes more straightforward. We're not going to turn our government into God's Kingdom, but we can encourage it to conform more fully to the mandate of God outlined by Peter.

As we noted in our previous study on Awakening, we're beginning to see how our families, workplaces, and our communities, culture, and society as a whole have deviated from God's ways. Our hearts yearn to see His Kingdom develop and grow in our midst. The Lord's Prayer is coming alive to us, and we graduate into the maturity of those who, after becoming personally cleansed and restored, seek to encourage positive changes, reforms, and even transformation to take place in those around us. Then with all the saints and host of Heaven we cry out: *"May your Kingdom come, your will be done, on earth as it is in Heaven!"*

Keeping our kingdom priorities with integrity

1. Review Jesus' Parable of the Hidden Treasure in Matthew 13:44. What does it mean to you to "sell all in order to buy that field"?

2. Are you getting a good grasp of what the Kingdom of God is all about or do you still have a lot of questions? List some.

Kingdom: God's Reign in our Midst

42

3. Is the current order of your civil government compatible or at odds
    with the principles of God's Kingdom? Explain your view.

4. Note some ways you might be able to advance the Kingdom of
    God in your midst or encourage your civil government to improve.

5. Do you think you've become either too active or too inactive in the
    governmental affairs of your community, state, or nation? If so, do
    you have a remedy in mind?

You may be interested in reading our handout by Michael Oh about
The Purpose and Role of Government for more Scriptural insights
about civil authority, online at www.celebratesalvation.org/more/#2.

Lesson 9E
Visions of the future

Understanding 6: To the Millennial Kingdom and Beyond:
Looking forward to Christ's second coming, millennial reign, and
final judgment while living in the realities of today's world.

Understanding eschatology – the prophetic word and biblical
timetable about the second coming of our Messiah – and what
we have to look forward to.

Matthew records a time when Jesus was asked by some Pharisees and
Sadducees to show them a sign from heaven:

> *He answered them, 'When it is evening, you say, 'It will be fair weather, for the
> sky is red.' And in the morning, 'It will be stormy today, for the sky is red and
> threatening.' You know how to interpret the appearance of the sky, but you cannot
> interpret the signs of the times.*
>   Matthew 16:2-4

In other words, "We can often read the signs of nature but may not
understand the prophetic words in our own Scriptures." This has been
especially true of understanding the plans God the Father has had for
the redemption of fallen mankind.

During the Roman occupation under Herod the Israelites were crying
out for their messiah to come with varying opinions about what he
would be like. Most were looking for a mighty man of valor who would
drive out the Roman oppressors and lead Israel into a time of fame and
fortune similar to that of Solomon's reign. Very few were anticipating a
humble suffering servant like the one depicted in Isaiah 53.

A close look at the Old Testament will reveal many passages that clearly
identify God's choice to be a very humble and unusual man like Jesus
(or *Yeshua*, meaning "salvation" in Hebrew). Closer study reveals that
not only will God's Messiah visit His people first as Savior with love,
wisdom, and demonstrations of healing compassion but He will return
later to vanquish His enemies and complete redeeming the earth with
mighty power as the Lord and King of heaven and earth.

Kingdom: God's Reign in our Midst

In addition to healing and teaching, Jesus had a lot to say as recorded in the New Testament about God's plans for the future. In keeping with many unfulfilled Old Testament prophecies, Jesus offered forgiveness and eternal life to all who would believe (trust) in Him and then to return personally to establish His Millennial Kingdom on earth. He listed several signs recorded in Matthew 24 before wrapping up with

So also, when you see all these things, you know that he is near, at the very gates.

His object was that we would be able to "*interpret the signs of the times*" and prepare for His arrival. Peter and Paul followed through with many other similar observations, capped off dramatically with the writings of John in his letters and remarkable prophetic visions and warnings in the book of Revelation. But have we been listening? Are we heeding Solomon's crucial admonition that instructs us to

Trust in the Lord with all your heart, and do not lean on your own understanding. In all your ways acknowledge him, and he will make straight your paths. Be not wise in your own eyes; fear the Lord, and turn away from evil. Proverbs 3:5-7

There are basically three views of the prophetic message the Bible has about "eschatology" or what will happen in the future to the world and its inhabitants. Due to human error and internal inconsistencies they have with the biblical record, they obviously can't all be correct.

Three interpretations of the prophesied millennial reign

Before completing Lesson 9E it's vital to read what Jesus, John, Paul, and Peter had to say directly about this subject, as assembled in our handout entitled **New Testament Eschatology**. A second handout essential for discussion of this Lesson, entitled **Prophetic Views of The Millennium**, is also available at www.celebratesalvation.org/more/#2.

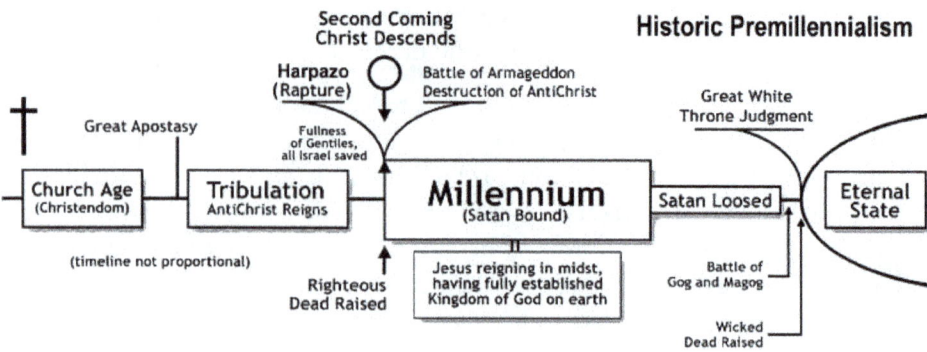

1. **Premillennialism** – This historic view, which predominated in the pre-Constantinian church, has come back into favor following the Reformation and especially since the profound disappointments of Enlightenment progressivism. It interprets the prophetic word literally and foretells a challenging timeline of history leading up to very troubling times of Great Tribulation just prior to the return of Jesus to establish the 1,000 year reign of His Kingdom on Earth.

2. **Amillennialism** – This view, promulgated as the Church became organized and rose in prominence in the 3rd and 4th Centuries, interprets end time prophecies in a symbolic rather than literal way. Instead of foreseeing a literal 1,000 year reign of Christ, it teaches that the millennium Jesus foretold started when He first came, is being manifested in the world more and more as the Church grows, and will culminate in final judgment when Jesus returns.

3. **Postmillennialism** – This interpretation, developed more recently and often held by eager believers during times of widespread revival, proposes that the world will get progressively better and better as the Kingdom of God becomes established through the spread of the Gospel, and then Jesus will return in person to rule over it.

Anticipating what lies ahead

1. What thoughts and imaginations does this brief review bring to your mind? What would you like to learn more about?

2. If you were to die suddenly tomorrow, where do you imagine you would find yourself?

3. As you contemplate the possibility of being part of Christ's Millennial Kingdom, where do you think you might fit in?

4. From your Bible reading on this subject, what thoughts do you have about how the Jewish people and Israel might fit in?

5. Are we getting closer to "the end"? Do you see any problems developing? If so, how should we be praying and acting now?

Reading our handouts **Five Reasons to Value Studying the End Times**, **New Testament Eschatology**, and **Prophetic Views of the Millennium** is really essential to understanding Lessons 9-12. All three are available at www.celebratesalvation.org/more/#2.

Understanding 6   Lesson 9E

Lesson 10E
Christ's millennial reign

Understanding 6: To the Millennial Kingdom and Beyond:
Looking forward to Christ's second coming, millennial reign, and final judgment while living in the realities of today's world.

Seeing the real world while imagining, praying, and working toward the ideal. Responding to Jesus' question, "when the Son of Man comes, will He find faith on earth?"

Developing substantial hope for the future

Eschatology is actually all about anticipating what we can expect in the future and learning how to be good stewards of His grace along the way. It's encouraging to think that the age of mankind will close with the fulfillment of God's promises, but what will that be like? As you may have noticed, our Kingdom study favors Historical Premillennialism as the most cohesive and helpful Scriptural perspective on the future, the one that gives us the best insights about how we should be living now.

From our 21st Century perspective it's difficult to believe that we will all become united in one Church before Christ returns as suggested by Amillennialism or be able to win our entire diverse and troubled world to the Kingdom ready to welcome Jesus back to usher us directly into our "Eternal State" as suggested by Postmillennialism without first experiencing the sovereign millennial reign revealed in Scripture.

The early enthusiasm of the Roman Church, encouraged by its organized unity and the secular embrace of the Empire, has become undermined by centuries of human error, worldliness, and division. Christendom, with all its art, cathedrals, music, and other evidences of cultural power, also appears to be less like a unified citadel and more like a host of sand castles, leaving Amillennialists more and more alone on the shore. Islam, Marxism, and doctrinaire secularism have overtaken large segments of the world's population that seem beyond even the most dedicated hopes of mountain-taking Postmillennialists. And if everything is to be in order when He returns as these two millennial views suggest, what are we to make of the question Jesus asked at the end of his parable of the persistent widow in Luke 18?

Nevertheless, when the Son of Man comes, will he find faith on earth?"

A short Question & Answer list drawn from Matthew 24

1. Will things be getting better and better leading up to Christ's return? No, quite the contrary (Matthew 24:3-8).. There will be ups and downs, times of encouragement and times of distress, and some very painful developments *("birth pangs")* including worldwide falsehood and wars that lead up to the Second Coming

2. Will believers experience tribulation before Jesus returns? Yes (Matthew 24:9-31). Think about what people have been enduring throughout history right up to now, including hunger, persecution, poverty, sickness, slavery, and war, and then try to tell all those who suffered that their experiences weren't tribulation.

3. Can we predict when Jesus will return with any accuracy? No (Matt. 24:32-44), but we can prepare for it with faith, hope, and joy.

4. Will everyone be saved no matter what they have done in this life? No (Matthew 24:45-51): He will bless those who are His servants.

I have said these things to you, that in me you may have peace. In the world you will have tribulation. But take heart; I have overcome the world... Count it all joy, my brothers, when you meet trials of various kinds, for you know that the testing of your faith produces steadfastness. And let steadfastness have its full effect, that you may be perfect and complete, lacking in nothing.

John 16:33 and James 1:2-4

And just as it is appointed for man to die once, and after that comes judgment, so Christ, having been offered once to bear the sins of many, will appear a second time, not to deal with sin but to save those who are eagerly waiting for him.

Hebrews 9:27-28

The Bible gives us a series of positive prophetic visions and graphic assurances (see handout by John F. Walvoord suggested on Page 50) of what the Second Coming will be like when Jesus arrives with us as part of His amazing welcoming party and establishes the earthly paradise of His Millennial Kingdom:

For the earth will be filled with the knowledge of the glory of the Lord as the waters cover the sea. Habakkuk 2:14

Between now and then we've been given the "heads up" in Matthew 10:16 and James 1:5-8 that the world is not always going to be kind and receptive to His Word but that He will provide us with the wisdom we will need as we trust Him in our hearts to help us carry out His Great Commission.

Things we can be doing with the Lord's guidance and power

And Jesus came and said to them, "All authority in heaven and on earth has been given to me. Go therefore and make disciples of all nations, baptizing them in the name of the Father and of the Son and of the Holy Spirit, teaching them to observe all that I have commanded you. And behold, I am with you always, to the end of the age."

Matthew 28:18-20

I charge you in the presence of God and of Christ Jesus, who is to judge the living and the dead, and by his appearing and his Kingdom: proclaim the word; be ready in season and out of season; reprove, rebuke, and exhort, with complete patience and teaching. For the time is coming when people will not endure sound teaching, but having itching ears they will accumulate for themselves teachers to suit their own passions, and will turn away from listening to the truth and wander off into myths.

2 Timothy 4:1-4

Preparing for Jesus' Second Coming

1. What ideas do you have about whether Jesus will *"find faith on earth"* when He returns? How can we work toward that here and now?

2. What if Jesus plans to call on you to help Him set up and serve in His Millennial Kingdom instead of going straight to "Heaven"?

Kingdom: God's Reign in our Midst

50

3. Have you spent any time imagining what it will be like to join Jesus in the clouds on His arrival? If so, what will happen next?

4. In Matthew 24 Jesus promises each *"faithful and wise servant"* that *"he will set him over all his possessions"* when He comes. Are you ready?

5. Do the promises of Christ's Second Coming inspire you to cry out wholeheartedly *"Maranatha! O Lord, come!"* (Revelation 22:20)?

You may appreciate studying our **Bible Timeline and Bookends** and **Millennial Scripture References** handouts as well as John Walvoord's article about the **Millennial Kingdom & Eternal State**, all available online at www.celebratesalvation.org/more/#2.

Lesson 11E
Final judgment

Understanding 6: To the Millennial Kingdom and Beyond: Looking forward to Christ's second coming, millennial reign, and final judgment while living in the realities of today's world.

The promise of the rainbow covenant of peace and its replacement with fiery trials leading up to tribulation and culminating in judgment.

Throughout human history the rainbow has been a dramatic natural phenomenon invested with symbolic meaning. In ancient Greek and Norse mythology the rainbow represented a bridge between the gods and earth. The first book in the Bible records the covenant God made with Noah after the Flood, marked by a "bow" in the clouds:

Never again shall all flesh be cut off by the waters of the flood, and never again shall there be a flood to destroy the earth... When I bring clouds over the earth and the bow is seen in the clouds, I will remember my covenant that is between me and you and every living creature of all flesh. Genesis 9:11, 14-15

In the last book of the Bible, John recorded an image he saw of Jesus seated on a throne and, among many other things, "*around the throne was a rainbow that had the appearance of an emerald*" (Revelation 4:3).

In the 20th Century the rainbow began making its appearance as a symbol of international peace and more recently as a symbol used extensively by popular movements in the West to reflect pride in diverse expressions of sexual identity and behavior. How well do these modern appropriations of biblical symbolism reflect God's Word and heart? Peter spoke about the danger associated with various latter day confusions like this in his second epistle:

But false prophets also arose among the people, just as there will be false teachers among you, who will secretly bring in destructive heresies, even denying the Master who bought them, bringing upon themselves swift destruction. And many will follow their sensuality, and because of them the way of truth will be

Kingdom: God's Reign in our Midst

blasphemed.... For they deliberately overlook this fact, that the heavens existed long ago, and the earth was formed out of water and through water by the Word of God, and that by means of these the world that then existed was deluged with water and perished. But by the same Word the heavens and earth that now exist are stored up for fire, being kept until the Day of Judgment and destruction of the ungodly. 2 Peter 2:1-2; 3:5-7

In the context of our study of biblical eschatology, questions arise about this *"Day of Judgment"* that Peter references. What will it be like, when will it come, and who will be affected? Reading the epistles of Peter and the last three chapters of John's Revelation is very helpful.

Beloved, do not be surprised at the fiery trial when it comes upon you to test you, as though something strange were happening to you. But rejoice insofar as you share Christ's sufferings, that you may also rejoice and be glad when his glory is revealed. 1 Peter 4:12-13

In the Premillennial view there will actually be a preliminary selection when Jesus comes back with His "Bride" to establish the Millennial Kingdom followed by a final judgment of the remainder before His *"great white throne"* in Revelation 20:11-15 at its close. In both Amillennial and Postmillennial views, however, *"the Day of Judgment"* will culminate at the end of the present or "church" age when they foresee the return of Christ occurring. In all 3 views, as wrapped up in Revelation 21, those who have lived for Christ will then inherit *"a new heaven and a new earth"* (aka Heaven) for eternity, while those who have not will be *"thrown into the lake of fire"* (aka Hell) for destruction along with the devil.

Speculations have been abounding ever since Jesus' first coming about the eternal destiny of mankind. Within a few centuries many of these were dramatically altered when Greek/pagan philosophy and integration into the Roman Empire were welcomed by the organized Church. It wasn't until the 16th Century that the role of faith in God's plan of salvation was revealed clearly again and began to be shared widely.

When Enlightenment rationalism emerged in the 18th Century it brought about profound challenges to foundational Christian understandings about the role of man's reason in determining truth, of final judgment in God's scheme of justice, and the very nature of God and Man. As reason began to overtake God's Word as the ultimate arbiter of truth, primary orthodoxies like the Divinity of Christ began to fade into Unitarianism and the possibility of eternal punishment to be absorbed into the concept of universal salvation. As a result, many areas of modern Western society like academia, the marketplace, and politics began to lose much of the influence orthodox Christian faith had in moderating secular humanism.

Perhaps the best way to address our current condition is to read the Word of God carefully and thoroughly and pray earnestly with the following idea of godly *"reason"* in the forefront of our minds:

> *"Come now, let us reason together," says the Lord: "though your sins are like scarlet, they shall be as white as snow; though they are red like crimson, they shall become like wool."*   Isaiah 1:18

As Christians we carry "bad news" of the reality, pervasiveness, and negative consequences of sin for those who refuse to acknowledge God's guidance and warnings. We also carry "Good News" about His free offer of forgiveness and cleansing from sin. With the Flood behind us and Christ before us, our choice is now between judgment by fire or repentance leading to eternal life. Let's choose abundant life and live it to the full in Christ while sharing His Good News whenever we can!

Approaching judgment with hopeful expectation

1. Are the symbolic interpretations of the rainbow found in the Bible compatible with those popularized by our current society?

2. From your reading of the Bible, what kinds of belief or behavior are incompatible with ultimate heavenly reward?

Kingdom: God's Reign in our Midst

54

3. How does someone obtain and hold onto eternal life? Try to summarize the Good News in a simple sentence or two.

4. What do you see as the primary differences between the three major eschatological views? Do they differ in judgment criteria?

5. As you look forward to the future and final judgment, list some goals and plans you have for your own personal growth in faith.

This would be a good time to read our handout on **The Messianic Church** and look up the Scripture passages that it references. If you can find the time, try to review as much of Matthew 23-25, the epistles of Peter, and the last three chapters of Revelation as well.

Lesson 12E
Anticipating our ultimate destiny

Understanding 6: To the Millennial Kingdom and Beyond: Looking forward to Christ's second coming, millennial reign, and final judgment while living in the realities of today's world.

Pursuing life-changing transformation from unexamined lives of sin to exemplary lives of deepening repentance, purity, integrity, and service.

In our last Lesson we began talking about inheriting the "*new heaven and a new earth.*" What will our lives be like leading up to the Millennial Kingdom, living through it, and moving on after Judgment Day?

Are we looking forward to anything and making preparations, or will we just let it happen? Have we adopted Doris Day's "que sera sera" ("what will be will be") attitude or are we being seriously proactive? If you recall her lyrics, the reason she gave for her attitude was because "the future's not ours to see." But what if the future IS ours to see? How would that change our outlook? Solomon warned us to seek God's vision for us:

> *Without receiving a progressive prophetic vision from God people tend to cast off restraint, wander away, and do their own thing, but those who seek, keep, and follow God's guidance will be blessed.* Proverbs 29:18 (author's version)

One way to approach the issue is to consider vocational retirement. You work hard at a job and raising your family but then, if you're fortunate to live long enough, your children have grown up (more or less) and it's time to retire from your job. Now what? Have you been looking forward to retirement and preparing for it, or do you just let it happen?

As my retirement approached, my wife and I began working out a plan with our co-workers, family, and fellowship some years in advance that involved financial arrangements, training others, and seeking the mind of Christ for His timing and what He was calling us to be doing next. The word we got was that He didn't want us to "retire" in the sense of pulling back into satisfying our own desires by doing our own thing. No, He wanted us to "graduate into retirement" by looking forward to applying

Kingdom: God's Reign in our Midst

our life's experience and learning in a variety of new family and faith endeavors in the community. He said, in effect, "Retirement isn't an end; it's a new beginning." The same is true for believers when we die! We're not going away; we're "graduating into eternity!" We're Christ's "*priests*" who are going to join our Lord in establishing His Millennial Kingdom!

For the Lord himself will descend from heaven with a cry of command, with the voice of an archangel, and with the sound of the trumpet of God. And the dead in Christ will rise first. Then we who are alive, who are left, will be caught up together with them in the clouds to meet the Lord in the air, and so we will always be with the Lord... To him who loves us and has freed us from our sins by his blood and made us a kingdom of priests to his God and Father, to him be glory and dominion forever and ever. Amen.

1 Thessalonians 4:16-17 and Revelation 1:5-7

His exact plan for us, whether we're still alive at His coming or have joined Him in our resurrected bodies, is beyond our knowledge, but when He comes we will know!

For now we see in a mirror dimly, but then face to face. Now I know in part; then I shall know fully, even as I have been fully known.

1 Corinthians 13:12

We can anticipate some things, however. We'll each have a vital place in His Plan. Harmony will prevail. Israel will be restored (Romans 9-11). There will be loved ones and saints we'll recognize, and hosts of other wonderful people to celebrate with (read Zechariah 14 and our handout **Festivals!**). The Millennial Kingdom will become more amazing as it unfolds in fulfillment of the Lord's Prayer for His Kingdom to come "*on earth as it is in heaven.*" And we'll be here for 1,000 years without sickness or death – imagine that compared to life you've been living so far!

Some speculate that we'll be "raptured" up and avoid tribulation while others suggest that we may be kept in a purgatorial "intermediate state" between our natural death and our resurrected lives to suffer a while for our sins. Jesus said we would all experience trials and tribulations in this life but that He died for our sins and with His death "*it is finished*"! Paul writes in 1 Corinthians 15 that we'll go right from physical death to resurrection life "*in a moment, in the twinkling of an eye*" and join up with Jesus as He's returning. And then, after our 1,000 years of Millennial Kingdom living on earth have run their course, our Enemy gets one more futile crack at us and our "ultimate destiny" unfolds. Our lesson?

Since all these things are thus to be dissolved, what sort of people ought you to be in lives of holiness and godliness, waiting for and hastening the coming of the day of God, because of which the heavens will be set on fire and dissolved, and the heavenly bodies will melt as they burn! But according to his promise we are waiting for new heavens and a new earth in which righteousness dwells. Therefore, beloved, since you are waiting for these, be diligent to be found by him without spot or blemish, and at peace. 2 Peter 3:8-14

It's all real, brothers and sisters. We'll be living right here on earth in His Millennial Kingdom and then in His amazing new heavens and new earth for eternity. Frankly, sometimes I can hardly wait.

How to keep focused and active between now and then:

1. **Pray** for His grace to abound and His Kingdom to come.
2. **Look** forward to participating in God's plans.
3. **Share** the Good News with family, friends, and neighbors.
4. **Disciple** and encourage believers in the Body of Christ.
5. **Grow** in maturity, insight, and knowledge of His will.
6. **Seek** the welfare of the community and nation where you live.
7. **Persevere** through challenging times with joy.

Preparing for life through and beyond the millennium

1. Are you praying for our Lord to come again and preparing to be a vital part of His Kingdom? What are some of your hopes?

2. How do you think that you and others can be fruitful during the time we have remaining?

58

3. What kind of support do you think would be helpful in equipping you and your congregation to handle tribulation?

4. Are you and your church preparing for what lies ahead? What plans do you have for meaningful study about the Kingdom of God?

5. In the light of eternity, what do you see as potentially effective ways to share the Good News with those around you?

The Spirit and the Bride say, "Come." And let the one who hears say, "Come." And let the one who is thirsty come; let the one who desires take the water of life without price. He who testifies to these things says, "Surely I am coming soon." Amen. Come, Lord Jesus! Revelation 22:17, 20

Commendation

Congratulations! You've just completed our study of what it is to be part of both the kingdoms of this world and the Kingdom of God. It's not easy to arrive at God's balance, but it's well worth the time spent in prayer, thought, and practice. The more we arrive at the goal of attaining "His righteousness" – that is, being rightly related to Him and our entire environment, including those around us – the more fruitful and joyful our lives will be.

Where do we go from here? As Mary Poppins might answer, "There's nowhere to go but up!" But how? Well, *"If God is for us, who can be against us?"* And if we can learn how to *"count it all joy as we encounter diverse trials"* which we've been told on very good authority will certainly come, then why not follow Corrie ten Boom's example and learn to manifest the entire list of the Holy Spirit's fruit in our lives along the way?

Our next study guide, ***Heaven: Our Ultimate Destiny***, will close out our Course 2 study series and take us across the final divide of time and space into the eternity of the new heavens and new earth where we will dwell in righteousness with the Lord forever in our glorified bodies.

How can we even imagine it? Our study will include casting a vision of what our lives and eternal home may be like during and after the close of the Millennial Kingdom, what the transition from here and now to there may involve, and how we can further prepare for and live out our amazing journey of faith between now and then.

In the meantime, by God's grace, may we continue meeting together to *"encourage one another, especially now that the day of his return is drawing near!"*

Kingdom: God's Reign in our Midst

Suggestions for Further Study

The Holy Bible
English Standard Version® ESV Study Bible™.

Corrie ten Boom – *In My Father's House: The Years Before "The Hiding Place."*

Gregg L. Frazer – *The Religious Beliefs of America's Founders: Reason, Revelation, Revolution.*

E. Stanley Jones – *The Kingdom of God: Is it Realism?*

Martin Luther King, Jr. – *Where Do We Go From Here: Chaos or Community?*

George E. Ladd – *The Gospel of the Kingdom.*

Esau McCaulley – *Reading While Black: African American Biblical Interpretation as an Exercise in Hope.*

Malcolm Muggeridge – *The End of Christendom but Not of Christ.*

John M. Perkins – *Dream with Me: Race, Love, and the Struggle We Must Win.*

Derek Prince – *The Beast or the Lamb: Discerning the Nature that Determines Your Destiny.*

Rose Publishing – *Four Views of the End Times: Christian Views on Jesus' Second Coming.* (as a pamphlet or in 2 longer versions)

Ed Silvoso
Ekklesia: Rediscovering God's Instrument for Global Transformation.

Thaddeus J. Williams
Confronting Injustice without Compromising Truth.

Additional Celebrate Salvation® Resources

Books in the Joy of Christian Discipleship Series

The Joy of Christian Discipleship Course 1
Established in 3 Stages and 7 Steps, a 36-week group study

1. **A - Saved!** *Rescued by Grace*
2. **B - Sanctified:** *Coming Clean with God*
3. **C - Sent:** *Becoming a Living Letter*

    Plus - Handouts and Worksheets *or* **Complete Course 1**

An 8-week Devotional Guide to 3 Stages and 7 Steps

4. **Essentials of the Christian Faith:**
    7 Steps to Abundant Life, an 8-week daily devotional guide

The Joy of Christian Discipleship Course 2
Equipped in 3 Realms with 7 Understandings, a 36-week group study for Christians who are established in their faith

5. **D - Awakening:** *The Triumph of Truth*
6. **E - Kingdom:** *God's Reign in our Midst* (this book)

    Kingdom Handouts *
    A Confession of Dependence (1E)
    Organization diagram drawing (2E)
    12 Kingdom Parables (3E)
    The Divine Obsession (6E) *and* Forbidden Fruit (7E)
    The Purpose and Role of Government (8E)
    Five Reasons to Value Studying the End Times (9E)
    NT Eschatology *and* Prophetic Views of the Millennium (9E)
    Bible Timeline/Bookends, Millennial Scripture References (10E)
    The Millennial Kingdom and Eternal State (10E)
    The Messianic Church (11E) *and* Festivals! (12E)[†]

7. **F - Heaven:** *Our Ultimate Destiny*

    Plus – Handouts and Worksheets or **Complete Course 2**

*Links to all Handouts in printable PDF form as well as Additional Resources can be found online at www.celebratesalvation.org/more/#2.

Another Kingdom Press Book by Dr. Morehouse
[†]**The Biblical Festivals,** *including A Passover Seder*

Kingdom: God's Reign in our Midst

Notes